W9-AUM-338

Portage Public Library
2665 Irving Street
Portage, IN 46368

# HAPPY BIRTHDAY, EVERYWHERE!

# HAPPY BIRTHDAY, EVERYWHERE!

## BY ARLENE ERLBACH

### ILLUSTRATED BY SHARON LANE HOLM

The Millbrook Press    Brookfield, Connecticut

PORTER COUNTY PUBLIC LIBRARY SYSTEM

Portage Public Library
2665 Irving Street
Portage, IN 46368

MAR 1 3 2001

DISCARD
PORTER COUNTY
LIBRARY SYSTEM

J 394.2 ERL    PORTER COUNTY
Erlbach, Arlene.
Happy birthday, everywhere
/
33410006097143

To the children of the world on their
special day, and to the Saturday critique
group for their support.

AE

To Ronnie and Jack, who always like a good party.

SLH

Published by The Millbrook Press
2 Old New Milford Road
Brookfield, Connecticut 06804

Copyright © 1997 by Arlene Erlbach
Illustrations Copyright © 1997 by Sharon Lane Holm
All rights reserved
Printed in the United States of America
Lib. ed. 5 4 3 2          Paper ed. 5 4 3 2 1

*Happy Birthday to You*, words & music by Mildred J. Hill and Patty S. Hill © 1935
(Renewed) Summy-Birchard Music. All rights reserved. Used by permission. Warner
Bros. Publications U.S. Inc., Miami, Fla. 33014

Library of Congress Cataloging-in-Publication Data
Erlbach, Arlene.
Happy birthday, everywhere / by Arlene Erlbach; illustrated by Sharon Lane Holm.
p.  cm.
Includes bibliographical references.
Summary: Describes birthday greetings and celebration customs from nineteen
countries with complete how-to-do-it descriptions of food, games, and crafts.
ISBN 0-7613-0007-4 (lib. bdg.)  ISBN 0-7613-0346-4 (pbk.)
1. Birthdays—Juvenile literature. 2. Creative activities and seat work—Juvenile
literature. [1. Birthdays. 2. Games. 3. Handicraft.] I. Holm, Sharon Lane, ill. II. Title.
GT2430.E75  1997
394.2—dc21  96-40402  CIP  AC

# CONTENTS

# ACKNOWLEDGMENTS

This book would not have been possible without the help of the following. Your help and time are very much appreciated.

Africa Books
Lolade Akintunde
Karen Arnold
The Australian Consulate
Roland Still and the Consulate
    General of Brazil
Simon Green and the British
    Consulate General
Jennie Burton
The Canada Club
The Canadian Consulate
    General
Joy Dudgeon
Noha Aboulmagd and
    the Consulate General
    of Egypt
Angelica Lisula and the Consulate
    General of Germany
The Embassy of Ghana and Safadzi
    Kwamie Bedzra

Eliot Goldstein and the Consulate
    General of Israel
The Consulate General of Italy
Caryn Liang
Instituto Mexicano del Seguro
Olga Tipton and the Consulate
    of the Netherlands
Kate Niyoshi
Al Peña
Carlota Casaca and the
    Consulate of Peru
The Peterson Family: Sharon,
    Charlie, Stina, and Kaj
Bella Resnikov
Maria Schniter
The Embassy of Sudan
Rita Thomas
Winnebago Tribal Office
Helen Wei
Jean Yusuf

# INTRODUCTION

If you're like most kids, your birthday is one of your favorite days of the year. You probably celebrate with a party, a cake with candles, and presents. If you do, you are following ancient customs.

Thousands of years ago birthdays were considered dangerous because they marked a change in the person's life. This might cause evil spirits to do harm. So people believed if friends and relatives visited them, they would help protect them. The use of noisemakers at birthday parties is probably an attempt to scare these evil spirits away.

The custom of candles on a cake originated with early peoples as well. Believing that many gods lived in the sky, people lit candles and torches when they prayed. They hoped the rising smoke would send their prayers to the gods so that they would be answered. When you blow out candles and make a wish, you are following a modern version of this ancient custom.

Not all children celebrate their birthday the same way. Children of different cultures have some very different birthday customs.

In this book you'll read about games, foods, and customs that make birthday celebrations fun all over the world. You might want to add some of these activities to your own birthday celebration to make it even more special.

Arlene Erlbach

# AUSTRALIA

Greeting: Happy Birthday

**Australians speak English, so their birthday greeting is the same as ours.**

Australia is located on the other side of the world. Its seasons are the opposite of those in North America. Australian children are enjoying summer during the North American winter. And when it's summertime in North America, it's a mild wintertime in Australia.

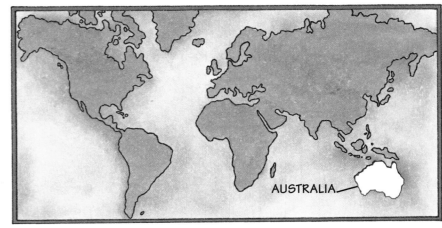

Because Australia's winters are not very cold or long, many Australian birthday parties are barbecues.

The children eat something called Fairy Bread. This popular snack is buttered bread covered with tiny, round, colored sugar sprinkles that are known as nonpareils. Another name for Fairy Bread is a Hundreds and Thousands Sandwich. The treat got its name because Australians call nonpareils "hundreds and thousands."

## Directions for making FAIRY BREAD

### What you'll need:

- slice of bread
- softened butter or margarine
- nonpareils (or regular sprinkles)
- knife

## What to do:

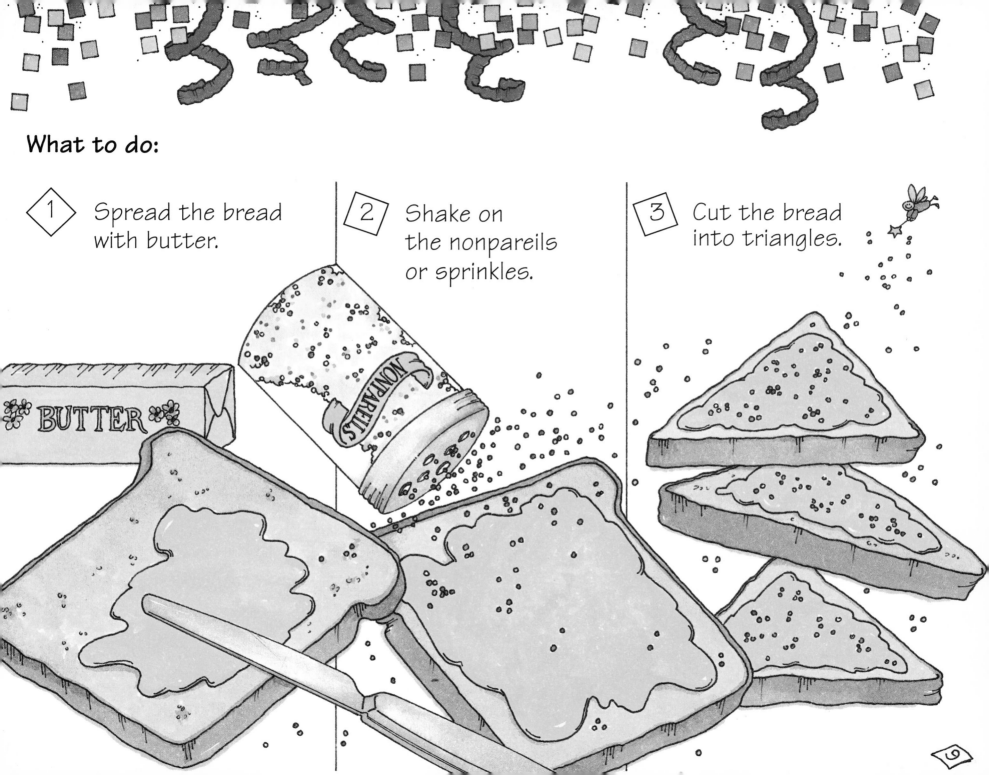

1. Spread the bread with butter.

2. Shake on the nonpareils or sprinkles.

3. Cut the bread into triangles.

BUTTER

NONPAREILS

# BRAZIL

Greeting: Feliz Aniversario, Feliz Aniversario
(Happy Birthday, Happy Birthday) Pronounced feh-LEEZ ah-ni-ver-SAH-ree-yo

**Although Brazil is located in South America where most people speak Spanish, Brazil's official language is Portuguese.**

How would you like to eat vegetables at your birthday party? Brazilian children do—in a way. Their families serve colorful candies shaped like vegetables and fruits. The candies are almost too beautiful to eat, and sometimes children take them home to enjoy for a while before eating them.

BRAZIL

Brazilians consider birthdays very special events. They decorate their homes with festive banners and brightly colored paper flowers. You will usually find some of these paper flowers on the party table, right by your plate. You can make these paper flowers for your own party.

## Directions for making PAPER FLOWERS

 ### What you'll need:

- six sheets of colored tissue paper for each flower
- three pipe cleaners for each flower

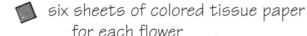

## What to do:

1. Place the sheets of tissue paper on top of one another.

2. Fold the papers like a fan, starting at the narrow end.

3. Tie the papers together tightly in the center with a pipe cleaner.

4. Now pull apart the paper layers. You'll have a beautiful flower.

5. Tie the bottom of the flower together with the second pipe cleaner.

6. Now attach the third pipe cleaner to make a stem.

# CANADA

Greeting: Happy Birthday

**Most Canadians speak English, so their greeting is the same as ours—unless you live in Quebec, where the official language is French, and then you say Bonne Fête (pronounced *bone fet*).**

At Canadian birthday parties many families serve homemade birthday cakes decorated with colored sugar sprinkles. Between the cake layers you might find a coin wrapped in wax paper. The guest who receives the piece of cake with the coin in it is the first to get a turn at all the party games.

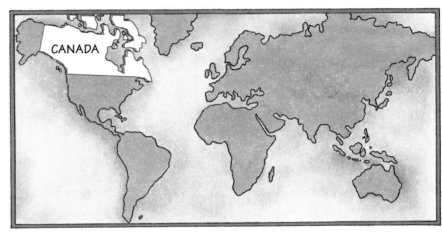

At Canadian birthday parties children receive colorful party favors called crackers. Crackers are cardboard tubes wrapped in crepe paper. They pop when you pull a paper strip. Inside you'll find a fortune, or a prize, or maybe even a party hat. Here's how to make something similar to crackers to give to your party guests.

## Directions for making CRACKERS

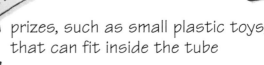

ALL OF YOUR DREAMS CAN COME TRUE! ☺

### What you'll need:

- [ ] one toilet-paper tube for each cracker
- [ ] crepe or tissue paper
- [ ] ribbon
- [ ] transparent tape

- [ ] prizes, such as small plastic toys, that can fit inside the tube
- [ ] fortunes written on strips of paper
- [ ] stickers

## What to do:

1 Place the cardboard tube at the narrow end of the paper.

2 Insert a prize.

3 Wrap the tube by rolling it in the paper.

4 When it's completely rolled, seal the seam with transparent tape.

5 Tie each end with ribbon.

6 To make your favors extra special, decorate with stickers.

At a Canadian birthday party guests sing "Happy Birthday to You" in English, unless they live in Quebec, where they sing it in French (see page 47).

13

# CHINA

Greeting: Sheng Ri Kuai Le (Birthday Greetings) Pronounced Shen rur Kway luh

**This greeting is in Mandarin, which is one of the languages spoken in China.**

CHINA

Many Chinese people don't celebrate the date they were born each year. Instead, each winter, during the Chinese New Year, every Chinese person turns a year older—no matter when his or her real birthday is.

Chinese people believe a baby is one year old when it's born. A Chinese child's second birthday (which would be your first) is an important event. Some families tell the baby's fortunes at this party. Actually the baby tells his or her own fortune! The parents seat the baby among a collection of objects, such as coins, a doll, or a book, and watch to see what object the baby grabs. A baby that grabs a coin might become rich. A baby that reaches for a book might become a teacher. A baby that grabs a doll might have many children.

The sixtieth birthday is also considered very important, and families often have big parties when somebody turns that age.

## How to play the CHINESE FORTUNE GAME

You and your friends can play a game similar to the Chinese second-birthday celebration. Set some objects on a table: a book, a pen, a spool of thread, a videocassette, a wooden spoon, a computer disk. Blindfold a friend and have him or her reach for an object. Here's what choosing some of these objects might forecast.

pen—a writer or journalist
book—a teacher or scholar
thread—a clothing designer or tailor
videocassette—a film producer
wooden spoon—a chef
computer disk—a computer specialist

You can make up fortunes, using any objects you choose. Remember, though, fortune-telling is just for fun. It doesn't really predict the future.

15

# ECUADOR

**The official language of Ecuador is Spanish.**

In Ecuador many children receive only a phone call on their birthday—or perhaps a card. Actual birthdays may not be much of a celebration at all. Most children in Ecuador are named for a saint, so they have a celebration similar to a birthday party on their saint's day.

Ecuadorian saint's day parties are usually afternoon tea parties. Hosts and hostesses serve raisin cake, fancy tea cookies, and hot chocolate. You can have a tea party with decorated cookies and hot chocolate on your birthday or any time of the year. Here's how to make decorated cookies similar to those served in Ecuador.

## Directions for making FANCY TEA COOKIES

### What you'll need:

- a roll of prepared sugar cookie dough
- knife
- cookie cutters
- lots of different-colored sprinkles, or colored sugar or tubes of colored frosting

# What to do:

1. Slice the cookies according to the package directions.

2. Cut them into shapes with the cookie cutters.

3. Decorate some of them with sprinkles or colored sugar.

4. Have an adult help you bake them according to the package directions.

5. Cool the cookies completely.

6. Frost the ones you didn't decorate with sprinkles or colored sugar.

7. Serve the cookies on a pretty plate.

# EGYPT

Greeting: (For a boy) Kulé Sana Winta Tayib (Every year I wish you good things) Pronounced koo-LEH SAH-na win-TEH tah-YIB, or (For a girl) Kulé Sana Wintie Tayyiba Pronounced koo-LEH SAH-na win-TEE tah-YIB-buh

**These greetings are in Arabic, the language spoken in Egypt.**

Egyptian people invite lots of friends and relatives to birthday parties, so they often serve two birthday cakes—one with candles and a second one without them. Cookies, individual cakes called gâteaux (gah-TOZ), sesame sticks, and small sandwiches on French bread complete an Egyptian party table. All the food, including the cake, is served at the same time.

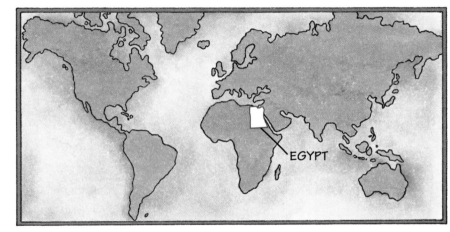

On birthdays Egyptian families often decorate their homes with paper garlands called zeena (ZEE-na) that look like chains of snowflakes. They hang the garlands all over the house, from wall to wall. You can make similar garlands and hang them up on your birthday. They'll make your house look very festive.

## Directions for making SNOWFLAKE GARLANDS

### What you'll need:

- sheets of paper or foil cut into squares
- scissors
- transparent tape

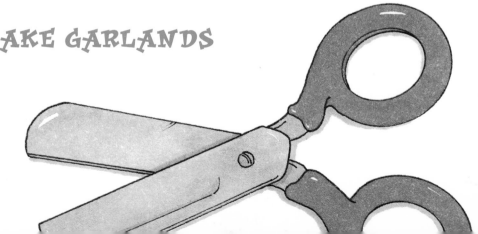

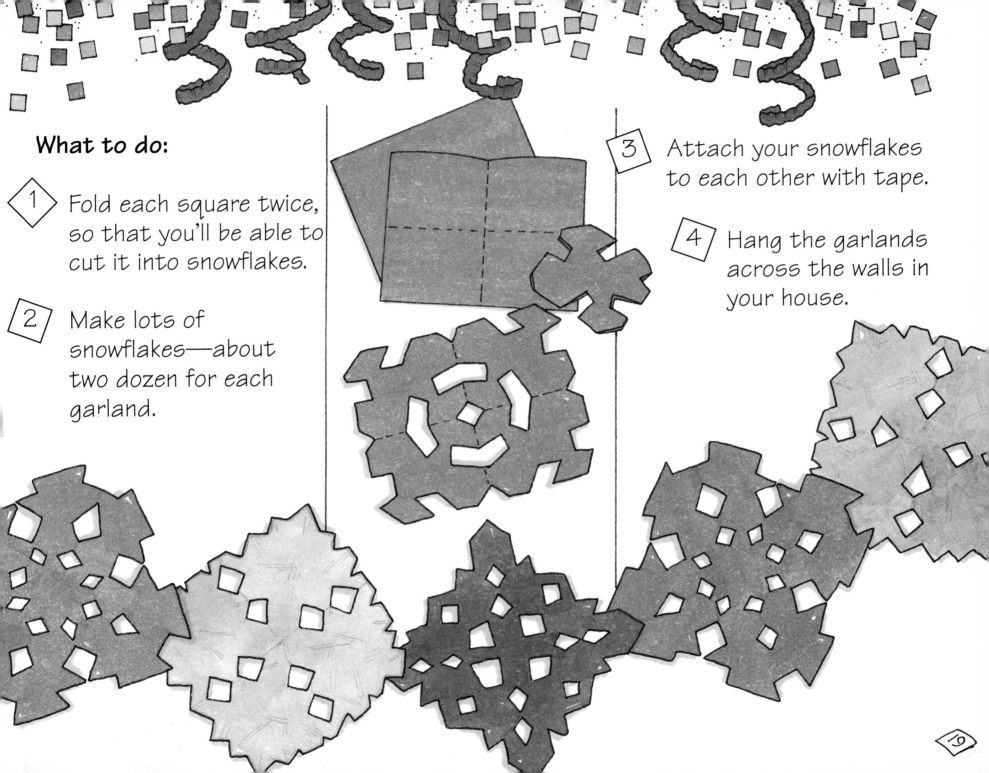

## What to do:

1 Fold each square twice, so that you'll be able to cut it into snowflakes.

2 Make lots of snowflakes—about two dozen for each garland.

3 Attach your snowflakes to each other with tape.

4 Hang the garlands across the walls in your house.

# GERMANY

Greeting: Alles gute zum Geburstag (All is good for your birthday)
Pronounced AH-les goot zoom geh-BURS-tahg

**The official language of Germany is German.**

German children don't receive homework on their birthday, and they don't do chores. Germans take birthdays very seriously, especially for kids. The custom of celebrating children's birthday parties began in Germany hundreds of years ago, and this tradition has spread around the world.

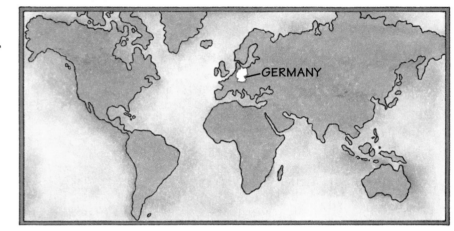

On a child's birthday German families often decorate their dining room or kitchen table with a special wooden birthday wreath. The wreath contains small holes for candles and a holder in the center for the lifecandle, which is taller than the other candles and beautifully decorated. The lifecandle is lighted each year on a child's birthday until the child turns twelve.

Make a lifecandle and burn it on your birthday—or give one to a friend for a birthday gift.

## Directions for making a LIFECANDLE

### What you'll need:

- a white 12-inch (30-cm) candle
- wax candle stickers (these can be purchased at a craft store)
- a permanent marker
- sequins
- sequin pins
- string
- ruler or tape measure
- scissors (to cut string, when measuring)

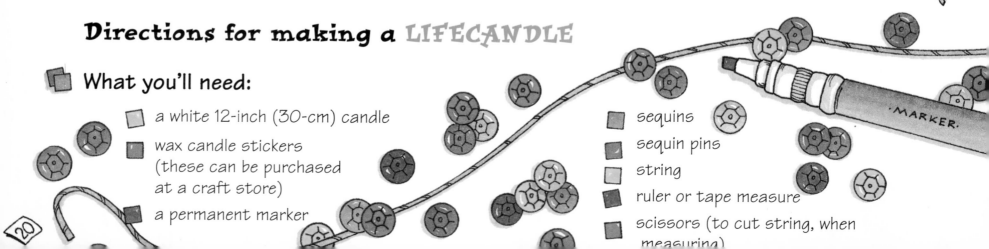

## What to do:

**1** Measure your candle so that you have 1 inch (30 cm) between each year, tying pieces of string around your candle to mark the measurements.

**2** Stick the sequins just above each piece of string, using the sequin pins. Then number with a permanent marker, 1 to 12, starting at the top of the candle. Remove the string before you light the candle.

**3** Decorate your candle with the wax candle stickers.

**4** The area between the sequins will be the amount you burn each year.

On your birthday burn your candle down to the next year's marking. The first year it may take a while—since you're starting with year one. Store your candle and use it again next year.

# GHANA

### Greeting: Happy Birthday

The official language of Ghana is English, although people speak many tribal languages. Here is how to say Happy Birthday in Ewe (pronounced Eh-vay), the tribal language of the Ewes of southeastern Ghana: Medzi dzigbe njkeke nyuie na wo (I wish birthday happy to you) Pronounced mehd-ZEE gih-BAY nuh-KAY-KAY new-EH nah woe

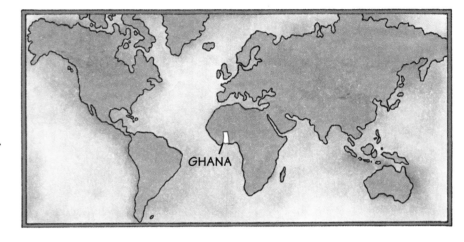

GHANA

In Ghana birthday children may wake up to a special birthday treat called oto (AH-toe). It's a patty made from mashed sweet potato and eggs and fried in palm oil. Later in the day children have a birthday party similar to yours, but they might eat stew and rice and a dish called *kelewele* (kelly-welly), which is fried plantain chunks. Plantains are similar to bananas.

　　At birthday parties Ghanaian children often play a very old native game called Ampe (AM-pay).

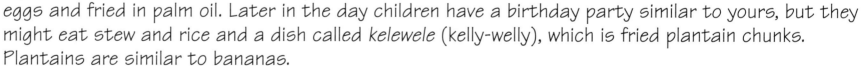

## How to play AMPE

### Number of players: 6 to 12

1　Children stand in a circle.

2　The birthday child is the leader and stands in the center.

3　The leader selects the first player and faces that child.

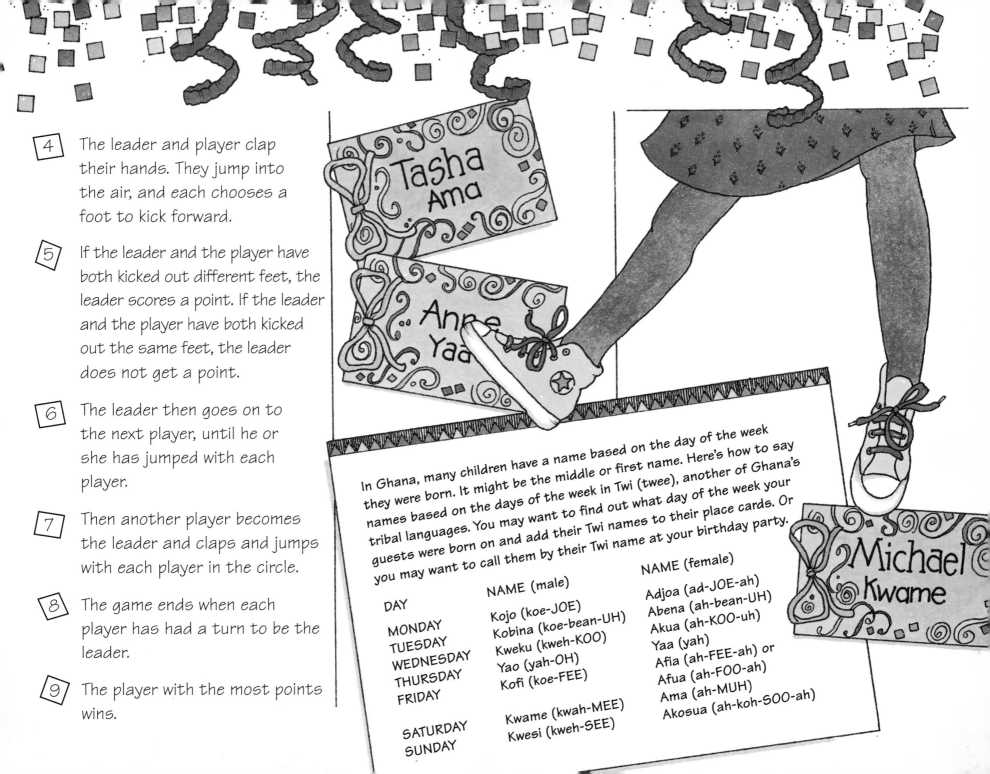

4 The leader and player clap their hands. They jump into the air, and each chooses a foot to kick forward.

5 If the leader and the player have both kicked out different feet, the leader scores a point. If the leader and the player have both kicked out the same feet, the leader does not get a point.

6 The leader then goes on to the next player, until he or she has jumped with each player.

7 Then another player becomes the leader and claps and jumps with each player in the circle.

8 The game ends when each player has had a turn to be the leader.

9 The player with the most points wins.

In Ghana, many children have a name based on the day of the week they were born. It might be the middle or first name. Here's how to say names based on the days of the week in Twi (twee), another of Ghana's tribal languages. You may want to find out what day of the week your guests were born on and add their Twi names to their place cards. Or you may want to call them by their Twi name at your birthday party.

| DAY | NAME (male) | NAME (female) |
|---|---|---|
| MONDAY | Kojo (koe-JOE) | Adjoa (ad-JOE-ah) |
| TUESDAY | Kobina (koe-bean-UH) | Abena (ah-bean-UH) |
| WEDNESDAY | Kweku (kweh-KOO) | Akua (ah-KOO-uh) |
| THURSDAY | Yao (yah-OH) | Yaa (yah) |
| FRIDAY | Kofi (koe-FEE) | Afia (ah-FEE-ah) or Afua (ah-FOO-ah) |
| SATURDAY | Kwame (kwah-MEE) | Ama (ah-MUH) |
| SUNDAY | Kwesi (kweh-SEE) | Akosua (ah-koh-SOO-ah) |

Tasha
Ama

Anne
Yaa

Michael
Kwame

# GREAT BRITAIN

**The official language of Great Britain is English.**

At a birthday party in Great Britain you'd have squash to drink. Squash isn't a vegetable drink, though. It's the British word for an orange- or lemon-flavored beverage like Kool-Aid made from syrup, rather than powder.

You'd have a cake with candles and chocolate biscuits, which are chocolate cookies. And you might have jelly and ice cream, which is gelatin with ice cream, maybe decorated with tiny balls of colored sugar. Here's how to make this very British party dessert.

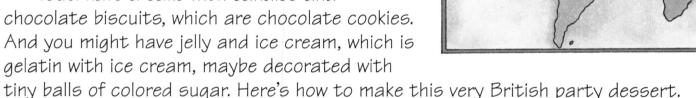

## Directions for making JELLY AND ICE CREAM

### What you'll need:

- one or two 4-serving packages of gelatin mix
- bowl
- spoon
- dessert dishes
- ice cream
- nonpareils (tiny colored sugar balls)

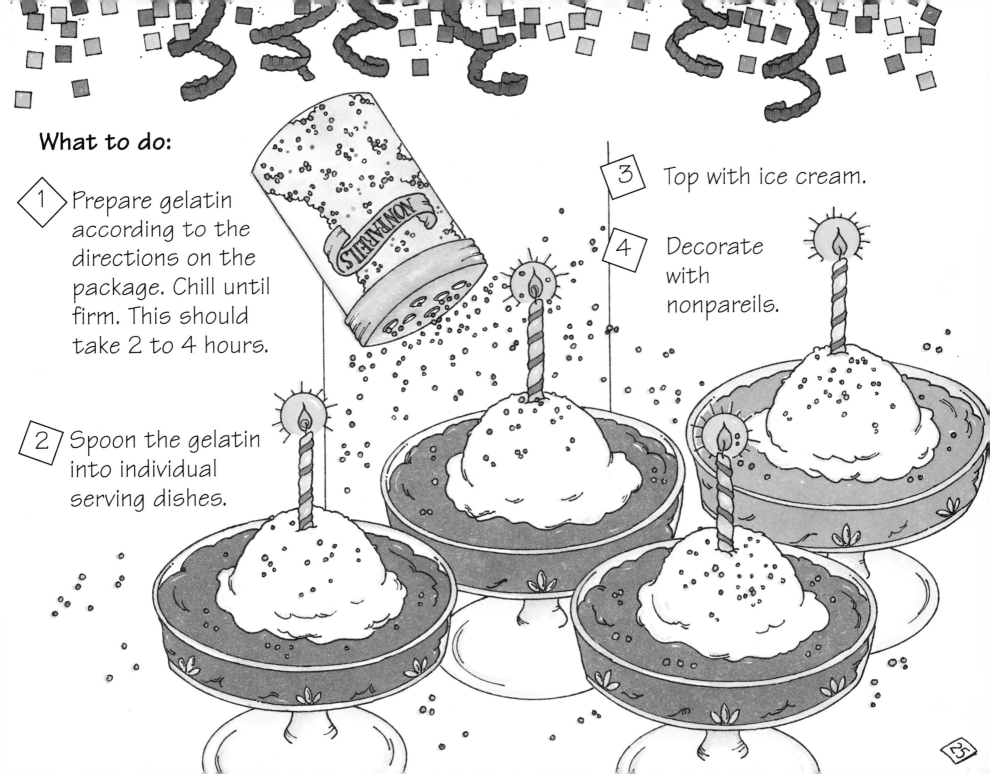

**What to do:**

1. Prepare gelatin according to the directions on the package. Chill until firm. This should take 2 to 4 hours.

2. Spoon the gelatin into individual serving dishes.

3. Top with ice cream.

4. Decorate with nonpareils.

NONPAREILS

# INDIA

Greeting: Sal Girah Mubarak (Happy Birthday)
Pronounced sal-GIH-rah-muh-BAH-rahk

**This greeting is in Hindi, one of the languages spoken in India.**

In India a child usually wears new clothes on his or her birthday. A birthday child may rise at sunrise and dress in the new clothes. Then the child kneels and touches the feet of his or her parents to show respect. Next, the family visits a shrine, where they pray, and the child is blessed.

In the afternoon the family might host a birthday meal that includes a spicy vegetable stew called curry, and chutney, a spiced fruit relish. For dessert the family serves a treat called *dudh pakh* (dude pock), which is similar to rice pudding. Indian people often stir in pistachios, almonds, raisins, and a spice called cardamon.

## Recipe for DUDH PAKH

### What you'll need:

- one or two 4-serving packages of prepared rice pudding mix
- bowl
- spoon
- 1 tablespoon cardamon
- pistachios, raisins, and almonds
- dessert dishes

**What to do:**

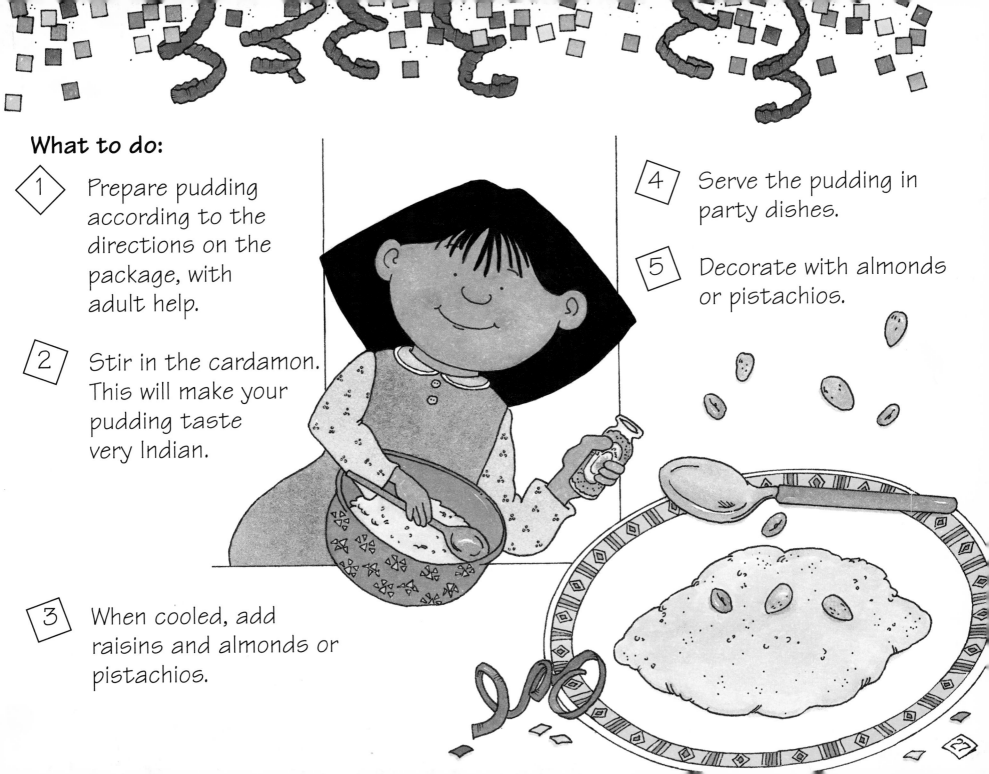

1  Prepare pudding according to the directions on the package, with adult help.

2  Stir in the cardamon. This will make your pudding taste very Indian.

3  When cooled, add raisins and almonds or pistachios.

4  Serve the pudding in party dishes.

5  Decorate with almonds or pistachios.

# ISRAEL

Greeting: Yom Holedet Sameach (May the day of your birth be happy)
Pronounced yome hoe-LEH-det sum-MAY-ahk

**The official language of Israel is Hebrew.**

In Israel, you might be considered a king or queen on your birthday. At some Israeli birthday parties, the birthday child wears a crown made from leaves or flowers and sits in a chair decorated with streamers. Party guests dance around the chair and sing. The child's parents lift the chair, while the child sits in it.

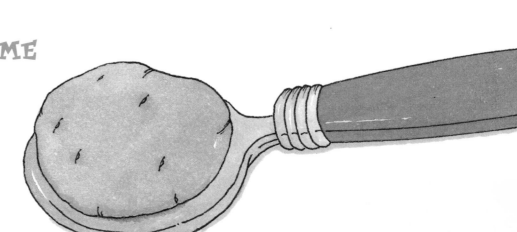

ISRAEL

After the singing everyone eats cake, usually shaped to represent the child's special interest. A dog lover will have a dog-shaped cake. A soccer player's cake will resemble a soccer field or soccer ball. A teddy bear collector's cake will look like a teddy bear.

After the refreshments Israeli birthday party guests usually have races or play games of skill. One race involves balancing a potato on a spoon. You can play this game on your birthday or anytime you have friends over to visit.

## How to play the POTATO GAME

### What you'll need:

- you need at least two players
- a spoon for each player
- a small potato that can fit on a spoon for each player

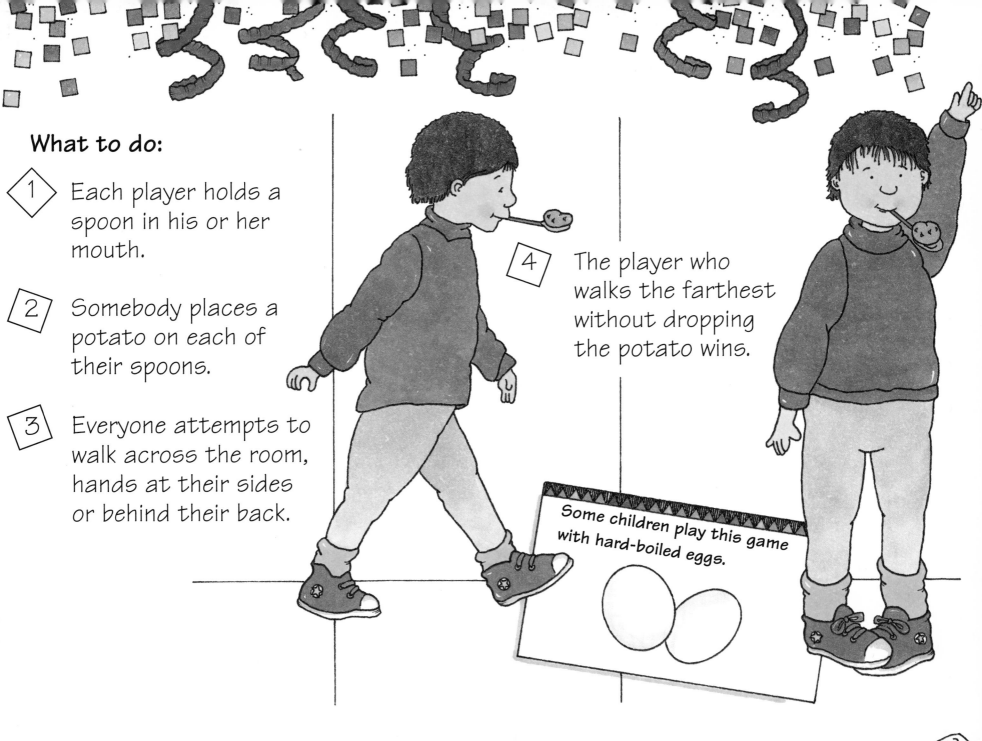

## What to do:

1 Each player holds a spoon in his or her mouth.

2 Somebody places a potato on each of their spoons.

3 Everyone attempts to walk across the room, hands at their sides or behind their back.

4 The player who walks the farthest without dropping the potato wins.

Some children play this game with hard-boiled eggs.

# MEXICO

**The official language of Mexico is Spanish.**

If you lived in Mexico you'd have two parties each year—your name day celebration and your birthday party. On a child's name or saint's day, the family attends church. A priest blesses the child. Then the family returns home for a party that includes relatives and very close friends. A saint's day party is usually quieter and a bit more formal than a birthday party.

Mexican children invite lots of friends to their birthday parties, which always feature a *piñata* (peen-YAH-tuh). A piñata is a decorated bag or jug, usually shaped like an animal. It's filled with candies, small toys, and coins. The piñata hangs from the ceiling, and blindfolded children attempt to break it with a stick. When it breaks, everyone scrambles to gather all the prizes. You can make individual piñatas and fill them with candy, coins, and small prizes, to be used as goody bags. Or fill the piñatas with shredded paper to be saved as a memento of your birthday party. You can even make them at your party as a special project.

## Directions for making INDIVIDUAL PIÑATAS

### What you'll need:

- [ ] wrapped candy, coins, and small toys to fill the piñatas, or they can be filled with shredded paper and not used as goody bags

- [ ] small paper lunch bags
- [ ] colored paper strips cut about 6 inches (15 cm) long and 1 inch (3 cm) wide
- [ ] a stapler

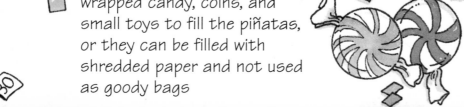
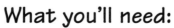

rubber cement

crayons or markers     scissors

## What to do:

1. Fold a piece of paper in half and draw an animal head, leaving a part of the head along the fold of the paper. Make a tail to go with the head. (Draw an animal pattern for each bag.)

2. Color the pattern. Then cut it out.

3. Cut the bag as shown in the picture.

4. Fill with candies, coins, and small toys.

5. Staple the bag shut.

6. Attach the head and tail with rubber cement.

7. Cut scallop edges on the paper strips.

8. Attach the strips to the piñata with rubber cement.

9. Put a piñata next to each guest's plate, or you may want to hang them across the room from a string or clothesline. An individual piñata filled with a special gift might make a nice birthday present for a friend.

33

# THE NETHERLANDS

**The official language of the Netherlands is Dutch.**

Dutch people consider birthdays very important events. In almost every Dutch home, you'll find a birthday calendar hanging in the bathroom! The calendar reminds everyone in the house about their friends' and relatives' special days. A birthday is usually acknowledged with a visit.

THE NETHERLANDS

Many Dutch children have a cake with candles at their birthday party, like ours. They may have pancakes sprinkled with powdered sugar, too. Dutch children also eat taartjes (tart-JEHS) on their birthdays, served with lemonade or hot chocolate.

Taartjes are small tarts made with many different kinds of fillings. You can make a treat similar to taartjes for your birthday party or any time friends visit.

## Recipe for TAARTJES

### What you'll need:

- individual tart shells or individual graham cracker crusts, available at most supermarkets
- instant pudding mix
- sliced fruit, such as strawberries or bananas
- whipped cream or dessert topping

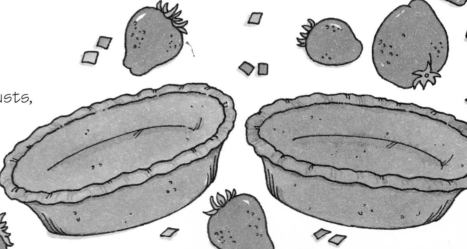

## What to do:

$\langle 1 \rangle$ Prepare pudding according to the directions on the package.

$\boxed{2}$ When the pudding is set, mix in the fruit.

$\boxed{3}$ Fill the tart shells with the pudding mixture.

$\boxed{4}$ Decorate with whipped cream or fruit.

In the Netherlands, a birthday child sits in a special chair decorated with lots of colored paper streamers, known as slingers.

# NIGERIA

All Nigerians speak English. Many speak a tribal language, too, like Ibo, Hausa, or Yoruba. Eku ojobi means Happy Birthday in Uruba.

In some Nigerian families the first, fifth, tenth, and fifteenth birthdays are considered special events. Families give huge parties. They might invite more than one hundred guests, both children and adults.

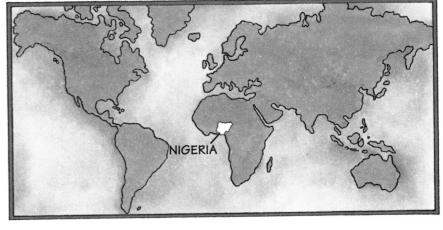

The birthday feast can include an entire roasted cow or goat. Families also serve *jollof* rice, a dish made from rice, tomatoes, red peppers, and onions, and *cassava* (kuh-SAH-vuh), which is similar to a sweet potato.

At Nigerian birthday parties, children often play a game called Pass the Parcel. Guests attempt to unwrap a package that has a prize at the bottom, while music plays in the background. Pass the Parcel is fun at any party or birthday celebration.

## How to play PASS THE PARCEL

 **Preparation:** Select a prize: a book, a small stuffed animal, an inexpensive electronic game, or lots of small prizes.

Wrap the main prize in many layers of newspaper. Tape each layer closed. If you're using smaller prizes, tuck them into the newspaper layers.

You will need a record player, CD player, or stereo, and somebody to play the music.

## How to play:

1. Everyone sits in a circle.

2. The person in charge of the music turns it on.

3. As the music plays, guests pass the parcel.

4. From time to time, the person in charge of the music stops it. Then the player holding the parcel when the music stops unwraps it until the music begins again.

5. The last player to unwrap the parcel keeps the prize.

You can make Pass the Parcel extra exciting. Include smaller prizes throughout the parcel. This way more guests have a chance to receive a prize.

# NORWAY

**This greeting is in Norwegian, the language spoken in Norway.**

If you visit a Norwegian home and see a chocolate cake with chocolate frosting and dishes of red gelatin covered with vanilla sauce, you can be pretty sure it's somebody's birthday. These treats are almost always served at Norwegian children's birthday parties. Long, thin, colored streamers and candy decorate the table.

At Norwegian birthday parties, guests may go fishing, but not for fish. They play a game called Fishing for Ice Cream, where everyone pulls up a frozen treat attached to a piece of string.

## How to play

## FISHING FOR ICE CREAM

### What you'll need:

- popsicles or ice-cream bars
- long pieces of string for a fishing line
- a spring-type clothespin

## What to do:

Most Norwegian homes have balconies. So the children stand on the balcony to pull up their treat. If your home doesn't have a balcony, your guests can fish from the top of a stairway or a porch.

⟨1⟩ Attach the clothespin to the string.

⟨2⟩ One by one, each guest holds onto the fishing line.

⟨3⟩ An adult stands below and attaches the ice cream to the string.

⟨4⟩ Then the child pulls it up.

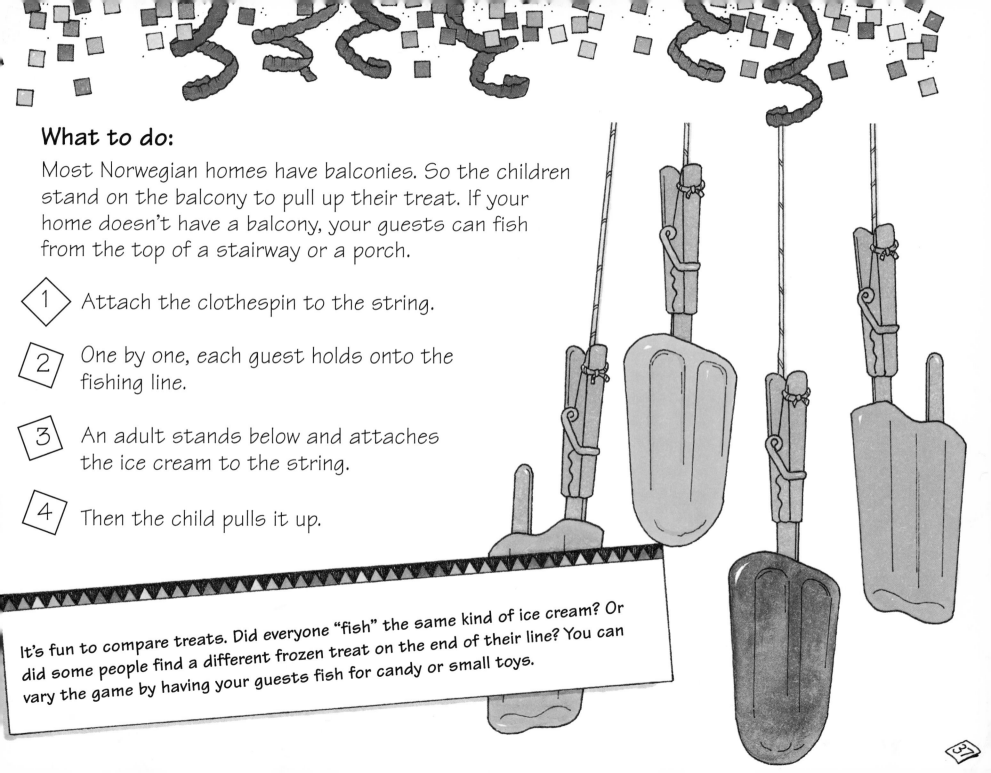

It's fun to compare treats. Did everyone "fish" the same kind of ice cream? Or did some people find a different frozen treat on the end of their line? You can vary the game by having your guests fish for candy or small toys.

# PERU

**The official language of Peru is Spanish.**

In Peru birthday party guests often receive two kinds of party favors. They call their favors *recordatorio* (reh-cor-dah-TOR-ee-oh), which means souvenir. One favor is a goody box or bag, similar to what North American children receive at a birthday party. The other type of favor is a pin made in honor of the event. The pins are so elaborate that some Peruvian children collect them.

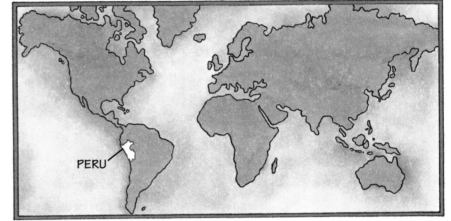

PERU

At Peruvian birthday parties children almost always receive fancy paper hats. The birthday child's hat looks like a crown, because he or she is the most special person of the day. You can make a crown for yourself or each of your guests. You can make a birthday crown for one of your special friends—or make crowns as an activity at your party.

## Directions for making a BIRTHDAY CROWN

**What you'll need:**

- yellow or gold construction paper
- rubber cement or transparent tape
- star-shaped foil stickers
- scissors

**What to do:**

1 Cut a crown strip in the shape shown below along the long edge of a piece of construction paper. Make another strip just like it.

2 Tape or glue the two strips together at each end to make a crown that fits around your head.

3 Decorate the crown with foil stars.

# RUSSIA

**The official language of Russia is Russian.**

If you lived in Russia you'd probably receive presents at school on your birthday. Teachers often give their students flowers, pencils, or books to celebrate their special day. Classmates may give small handmade gifts, too.

After school or on the weekend, a Russian child usually has a birthday party at home. The family might serve birthday cake or a birthday pie, with the greeting pricked into the crust. In Russia the birthday child, not the guests, gets the first slice of pie or cake.

At Russian parties children sometimes play a game that features a clothesline. Guests don't jump with it, though. The host or hostess hangs prizes on it, and everyone cuts off a prize to take home.

## How to play the CLOTHESLINE GAME

### What you'll need:

- a long rope that you can hang across the party room
- small prizes like pogs, baseball cards, plastic boats, animals, or dolls
- lunch bags
- string
- scissors
- blindfold

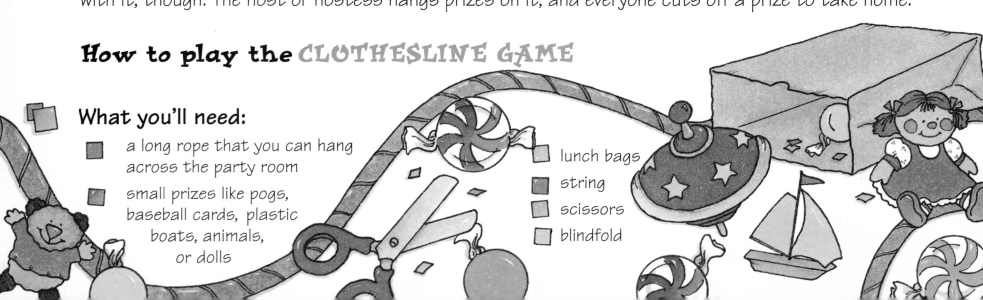

## What to do:

1. Hang the clothesline across the room.

2. Place the prizes in the lunch bags. You may want to decorate the bags first.

3. Twist the bags and tie tightly with string.

4. Tie the bags to the rope.

5. Blindfold each guest. Lead them to the clothesline.

6. Let each guest choose the bag that he or she wants.

7. Have an adult help snip the bag off the clothesline.

# SUDAN

Greeting: Aid Milad Jamil (Day of Birth Beautiful)
Pronounced aid mil-LAD JAH-mil

Sudanese people speak English and Arabic. Aid Milad Jamil is the greeting used in the dialect of Arabic spoken in Sudan.

In Sudan children living in rural areas usually don't celebrate birthdays, but children in cities do. They often have a cake with candles. They eat pizza and drink a red punch called karkady (car-KUH-day). It's made from hibiscus flowers.

At a Sudanese birthday party, children may not receive gifts like toys or clothes. Friends and family may give money, instead. After the food is served, children play lots of games. One of them may be The Sheep and the Hyena.

## How to play THE SHEEP AND THE HYENA

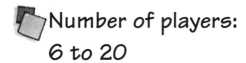Number of players:
6 to 20

**What to do:**

1. The birthday child chooses one guest to be the sheep, and another to be the hyena.

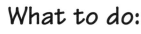

2. The other players form a circle.

3. The sheep goes into the center of the circle.

4. The hyena stays outside the circle.

5. The players move around in a circle.

6. They try to stay close to each other so that the hyena can't enter the circle and tag the sheep.

7. When the hyena enters the circle, he or she becomes the sheep.

8. Now another player is chosen to be the hyena.

9. The game ends when everyone has had a turn to be the hyena.

# UNITED STATES
## NATIVE AMERICAN— WINNEBAGO TRIBE

Greeting: Haptee Hocuenera Hinigiren (It's your Birthday) Pronounced Hahp-TEE hoe SUE-nyaira (rhymes with era) hih-nih-GIH-ren

**The language of the Winnebago Indians is Ho-Chunk.**

Winnebago Indians often have big birthday parties—anyone can attend. The invitation is spread by word of mouth. The party usually begins in the evening and can last all night.

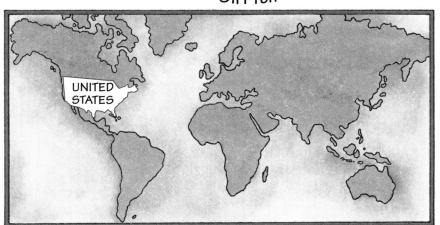

Whatever the birthday person wants to eat will usually be served at a Winnebago birthday party—even if it's something difficult to obtain like deer meat with gravy. Winnebago Indians feel that it's important to please a birthday person. The birthday cake is a very large sheet cake and is carried around and shown to the guests. It's considered to be a great honor to be asked to cut the cake.

After the meal children often play hand games. An adult holds a bone or stone in one of his or her hands and children try to guess where it is. Hand games are fun to play at birthday parties or any time you have a group of friends over. Here's a simplified version of a Native American hand game.

## How to play a NATIVE AMERICAN HAND GAME

 **What you'll need:**

 A stone or bone, which you can decorate if you like

44

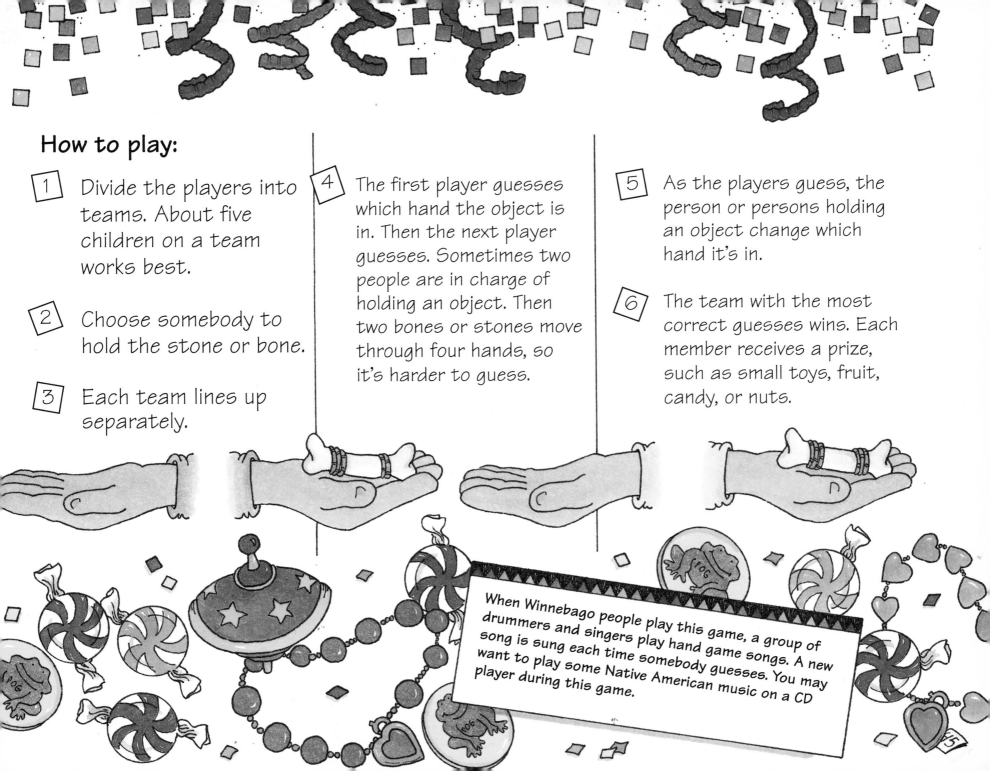

## How to play:

1. Divide the players into teams. About five children on a team works best.

2. Choose somebody to hold the stone or bone.

3. Each team lines up separately.

4. The first player guesses which hand the object is in. Then the next player guesses. Sometimes two people are in charge of holding an object. Then two bones or stones move through four hands, so it's harder to guess.

5. As the players guess, the person or persons holding an object change which hand it's in.

6. The team with the most correct guesses wins. Each member receives a prize, such as small toys, fruit, candy, or nuts.

When Winnebago people play this game, a group of drummers and singers play hand game songs. A new song is sung each time somebody guesses. You may want to play some Native American music on a CD player during this game.

# HAPPY BIRTHDAY TO YOU!

The song "Happy Birthday to You" was written in the United States more than one hundred years ago. It is sung in many countries of the world, sometimes in English and sometimes in the native language. Here are the words for "Happy Birthday to You" in some other languages.

Words and music by Mildred J. Hill and Patty S. Hill

## FRENCH

Bonne Fête A Tu
(Bone Fet Ah Too)

Bonne Fête A Tu
(Bone Fet Ah Too)

Bonne Fête A
(Bone Fet Ah) _____
name of person celebrating the birthday

Bonne Fête A Tu
(Bone Fet Ah Too)

## GERMAN

Züm Gebürstag Viel Glück
(Zoom Geh-BURS-tahg Feel Glook)

Züm Gebürstag Viel Glück
(Zoom Geh-BURS-tahg Feel Glook)

Züm Gebürstag Viel Glück
(Zoom Geh-BURS-tahg Feel Glook)

Züm Gebürstag Viel Glück
(Zoom Geh-BURS-tahg Feel Glook)

## KOREAN

Sang-il Chookha-Hapneeda
(Sang-ILL CHEW-kuh Hop-NEE-duh)

Sang-il Chookha-Hapneeda
(Sang-ILL CHEW-kuh Hop-NEE-duh)

Jul Guh Woon Sang-il Ulh
(person's name-eh)
(Jul guh woon sang-IL ull)

Chookha-Hapneeda
(CHEW-kuh Hop-NEE-duh)

## SPANISH

Cumpleaños Feliz
(Coom-plee-ON-yoes Feh-LEEZ)

Cumpleaños Feliz
(Coom-plee-ON-yoes Feh-LEEZ)

Cumpleaños Cumpleaños
(Coom-plee-ON-yoes Coom-plee-ON-yoes)

Cumpleaños Feliz
(Coom-plee-ON-yoes Feh-LEEZ)

## HEBREW

Yom Holedet Sameach
(Yome Hoe-LEH-det Sum-MAY-ahk)

Yom Holedet Sameach
(Yome Hoe-LEH-det Sum-MAY-ahk)

Yom Holedet Sameach
(Yome Hoe-LEH-det Sum-MAY-ahk)

Yom Holedet Sameach
(Yome Hoe-LEH-det Sum-MAY-ahk)

## ARABIC

Sana Helwa Ya Jamil
(Sah-NA HEL-wah Yah JAH-mil)

Sana Helwa Ya Jamil
(Sah-NA HEL-wah Yah JAH-mil)

Sana Helwa Ya
(Sah-NA HEL-wah Yah)

_____
name of person celebrating the birthday

Sana Helwa Ya Jamil
(Sah-NA HEL-wah Yah JAH-mil)

## PORTUGUESE

Feliz Aniversario Para Voce
(Feh-LEEZ On-nih-ver-SAH-ree-yo PAR-a VOE-say)

Feliz Aniversario Para Voce
(Feh-LEEZ On-nih-ver-SAH-ree-yo PAR-a VOE-say)

Feliz Aniversario Para Voce
(Feh-LEEZ  On-nih-ver-SAH-ree-yo PAR-a VOE-say)

Feliz Aniversario Para Voce
(Feh-LEEZ  On-nih-ver-SAH-ree-yo PAR-a VOE-say)

## ITALIAN

Buon Compleanno a te,
(Bwon cohm-play-ON-noe ah tay)

Buon Compleanno a te,
(Bwon cohm-play-ON-noe ah tay)

Buon Compleanno cara
(Bwon cohm-play-ON-noe cah-ROH)

boy's name _____

girl's name _____ caro

caro

cara

(Bwon cohm-play-ON-noe cah-RAH)

Buon Compleanno a te
(Bwon cohm-play-ON-noe ah tay)

47

# BIBLIOGRAPHY

Arnold, Caroline: *Everybody Has a Birthday*, Franklin Watts, New York, 1987.

Gibbons, Gail: *Happy Birthday!*, Holiday House, New York, 1986.

Johnson, Lois S.: *Happy Birthdays Round the World*, Rand McNally & Company, Chicago, 1963.

Milord, Susan: *Hands Around the World*, Williamson Publishing, Charlotte, VT, 1992.

Perl, Lila: *Candles, Cakes, and Donkey Tails*, Clarion Books, New York, 1984.

Price, Christine: *Happy Days*, United States Committee for UNICEF, United Nations, New York, 1969.

Rinkoff, Barbara: *Birthday Parties Around the World*, M. Barrows & Company, Inc., New York, 1967.